D1456673

A CHRISTMAS DEVOTIONAL FROM CHRISTIANITY TODAY

JOURNEYING THROUGH ADVENT WITH OUR HUMBLE & MIGHTY SAVIOR

CT

THE ETERNAL KING ARRIVES: A Christmas Devotional from Christianity Today

Christianity Today, 465 Gundersen Dr., Carol Stream, IL 60188
ChristianityToday.com

Printed in the USA

EDITOR Conor Sweetman
EDITOR IN CHIEF Russell Moore
CREATIVE DIRECTOR Sarah Gordon

DESIGNER Alecia Sharp
ILLUSTRATIONS BY Phil Schorr
PRODUCTION Rick Szuecs

COPY EDITING BY
Alexandra Mellen
Sara Kyoungah White

CONTENTS

For to us a child is born,
to us a son is given,
and the government will be on his shoulders.
And he will be called
Wonderful Counselor, Mighty God,
Everlasting Father, Prince of Peace.

ISAIAH 9:6

INTRODUCTION

Welcome to the season of Advent. It's a special time in the Christian calendar—one that we all want to take heed of, with its deep and lasting significance, even in the midst of the season's sometimes overwhelming demands. As you and your family approach a time of full calendars and bustling kitchens, candlelit services and living rooms strewn with wrapping paper, we invite you to journey through the season with this Advent devotional.

This devotional is meant to help you dive deep into theological truths and personal revelations as we prepare to celebrate the arrival of our humble and glorious King. We have structured the devotional to help us ponder the glory and tenderness of Christ, who came in the form of a vulnerable baby and displayed a gentle love for his creation through his incarnation. Throughout the month of December, we will herald both the sovereignty and power of his kingship and his self-emptying lovingkindness.

First, we will immerse ourselves in the prophetic inauguration of Christ, with devotionals that speak to the hopeful yearnings of Israel for the promised King—and the signs that would accompany his revival—woven throughout the Old Testament. Next, we will celebrate the eternal jubilee that Jesus' incarnation heralds: a time of freedom, joy, and new life that he now offers. Finally, we will draw near to Christmas Day by gazing in awe at Christ's royal enthronement and the establishment of his kingdom. He is our long-awaited Savior, and this Advent we celebrate the life-changing truth that our eternal King has arrived. **CT**

READING PLAN

WEEK 1 OF ADVENT

DAY 1 MICAH 5:2-5
Alexis Ragan: The Humble Character of Our King

DAY 2 JEREMIAH 23:5-6
Elizabeth Woodson: Prophesying a Perfect Ruler

DAY 3 ISAIAH 7:10-14
Alexandra Hoover: A Relentless Love

DAY 4 LUKE 2:22-32
Monty Waldron: An Unscheduled Appointment

DAY 5 LUKE 4:16-21
Kristel Acevedo: The Synagogue Visit That Changed Everything

DAY 6 ISAIAH 35:4-10
Beca Bruder: He Is Not One to Leave Us Hurting

WEEK 2 OF ADVENT

DAY 1 JOHN 16:33
Strahan Coleman: The Good News About Our Bad News

DAY 2 JOHN 3:16-21
Ronnie Martin: A Universe-Sized Love

DAY 3 2 CORINTHIANS 3:17-18
Steve Woodrow: How to Behold the Glory

DAY 4 1 PETER 2:9
Elizabeth Woodson: We Forget We Belong to God

DAY 5 JOHN 3:25-30
Laura Wifler: The Goodness of Growing Smaller

DAY 6 EPHESIANS 1:15-23
Carlos Whittaker: True Hope Cannot Be Manufactured

He said to them,
"Go into all the world
and preach the gospel
to all creation."

MARK 16:15

CONTRIBUTORS

Kristel Acevedo

Kristel Acevedo is an author, Bible teacher, and the spiritual formation director at Transformation Church just outside Charlotte, NC.

Dorothy Bennett

Dorothy Bennett holds a master's in theology and art from the University of St Andrews. She currently co-runs a video marketing company in Austin, TX.

Beca Bruder

Beca Bruder is the managing editor of *Comment* magazine.

Joy Clarkson

Joy Clarkson is a writer, editor, and doctoral candidate in theology. She is the books and culture editor at *Plough*.

Strahan Coleman

Strahan is a writer, musician, and spiritual director from Aotearoa, New Zealand. He has authored three devotional prayer books including the recently released *Beholding*.

Caroline Greb

Caroline Greb is a wife, mother, homemaker, fine artist, and the assistant editor at *Ekstasis Magazine*.

CONTRIBUTORS

Malcolm Guite

Malcolm Guite is a former chaplain and Life Fellow at Girton College, Cambridge. He teaches and lectures widely on theology and literature.

Alexandra Hoover

Alexandra Hoover is a wife, mother of three, speaker, ministry leader, and best-selling author of *Eyes Up: How to Trust God's Heart by Tracing His Hand.*

Ronnie Martin

Ronnie Martin is lead pastor of Substance Church in Ashland, OH. He also serves as director of leader renewal for Harbor Network and is the author of seven books.

Trillia Newbell

Trillia Newbell is the author of several books including *52 Weeks in the Word.* She is the radio host of *Living by Faith* and the acquisitions director at Moody Publishers.

Jon Nitta

Jon Nitta is the pastor of spiritual formation, discipleship, and small groups at Calvary Church in Valparaiso, IN.

Alexis Ragan

Alexis Ragan is a creative writer and ESL instructor, passionate about global missions.

Craig Smith

Craig Smith is the lead pastor of The Vail Church.

Monty Waldron

Monty Waldron is married with four children and started Fellowship Bible Church in 2000.

Carlos Whittaker

Carlos Whittaker is a storyteller, speaker, and author of *Moment Maker*, *Kill the Spider*, *Enter Wild*, and his latest release, *How to Human*.

Laura Wifler

Laura Wifler is a writer, podcaster, and cofounder of Risen Motherhood. She has authored several books for children, including *Any Time, Any Place, Any Prayer.*

Steve Woodrow

Steve Woodrow has been the teaching and directional Pastor at Crossroads Church Aspen, CO, for the past 23 years.

Elizabeth Woodson

Elizabeth Woodson is a Bible teacher, theologian, author, and the founder of The Woodson Institute, an organization that equips believers to grow in their faith.

We wait for the blessed hope—the appearing of the glory of our great God and Savior, Jesus Christ.

TITUS 2:13

PROPHETIC INAUGURATION

READ
MICAH 5:2-5

The Humble Character of Our King

BOLD PROCLAMATIONS OF A GREAT LEADER

BY ALEXIS RAGAN

As we read through the Old Testament prophecies of Scripture, we are reminded that it has always been set in stone that an everlasting ruler would emerge from Bethlehem. Micah 5:2 proclaims, as if announcing from the rooftops to reach the ears of the city, "Out of you will come for me one who will be ruler over Israel, whose origins are from of old, from ancient times."

With this bold proclamation, it's clear that God designed the news of this birth not to be kept a secret but to be spread throughout the land with confidence. Yes, *the* Anointed One, told to be trickling down from the Davidic line, was indeed coming, to save Israel from what they could not bear themselves. Imagine what waiting felt like during the prophets' times—the Ancient of Days was on his way, after all. Curious believers and dreamers alike must have lived with great anticipation. *What will this King be like? What wisdom,* they might have wondered, *will he bless us with to then carry us out of exile?* How would this King make himself known when he finally did come?

In keeping with his nature, Jesus takes on the mantle of a chief shepherd who graces his sheep with the sweet presence of strength and safety. There is something deeply calming about having a Savior who guides me like a shepherd does sheep—in the way I should go instead of the way I imagine best. We are all "prone to wander" from the safe path and away from his heart, as the hymn "Come Thou Fount of Every Blessing" puts it so vulnerably.

The Shepherd would cover Israel with his disposition of majesty and honor in the Father's name. He would stand steadfast as the ultimate overseer of their lives, ushering them bravely and boldly into everlasting pastures. This was something God's people not only longed for but desperately needed—a safe haven that would provide them rest. Micah 5:4 reassures us of the holy safeguard Christ will bring: "And they will live securely, for then his greatness will reach to the ends of the earth."

As his sheep, we have been given a bountiful lot of prosperity and protection. What's more, inhabitants of this land will find that the Chief Shepherd "will be our peace" (v. 5). What does this look like? We might imagine a herd of docile sheep resting freely under a shady tree as he stands with staff in hand, ensuring total serenity in his care. His peace ushers eternal shalom into every avenue of life. Not even Israel's opposing forces of Assyria on all fronts would be able to penetrate the gate (v. 5). Truly, there is no safer place than to be wrapped up in the loving ownership of our Creator to flourish in fields, unthreatened forever.

REFLECT

How does the humble character of our King challenge our understanding of God's mysterious plans?

In what ways does embracing Jesus as our Chief Shepherd transform our daily lives and relationships?

READ
JEREMIAH 23:5-6

Prophesying a Perfect Ruler

STARTLING PROMISES ON THE PERFECTION OF POWER

BY ELIZABETH WOODSON

Jeremiah was a prophet to people who were experiencing political turmoil. For years, Judah had been ruled by evil kings, men whose reigns were characterized by greed, idolatry, and injustice. Instead of caring for the people, they oppressed them. Jeremiah invited them to remember the covenant and shepherd God's people. Instead of imitating the nations around them, he called the kings to be different, to show the nations how to worship the one true God. But they ignored Jeremiah's warnings. Again and again, the kings chose their sin over God, and the people suffered. Amid this season of chaos, God was not silent. Through Jeremiah, he called out the inadequacy and failure of Judah's leadership. His words lobbed incriminating charges against those whose authority was not final but merely derived from the Sovereign One. The kings had forgotten they were stewards, appointed to care for a people who belonged to God.

Then, in Jeremiah 23:5–6, the prophet shared a startling promise. God was not going to do away with Judah's theocracy. He was going to perfect it. From David's family line, God would raise up a "righteous Branch," a rightful heir to the throne. This king would do what Judah's kings could not do—lead in a way that perfectly reflected God's justice and righteousness. Under his rule, the people would thrive and God would be worshiped. This king would save the people from their oppression.

But this king would not be another human king. This king would be God the Son, Jesus.

With words full of hope, the prophet reminded the people that God had not forgotten them. He had not turned a blind eye to their suffering. Rather, he was preparing the way for their suffering to end. Out of love, God the Father would send God the Son into the world to save it from the root issue that plagued both Judah and its kings—sin. Under the reign of Jesus, sin will be no more. He will right what is wrong, punish evil, and bring about equality for all. Humanity will be treated with justice and will reflect the righteousness of God. Jesus will restore the shalom that sin has disrupted and tries to destroy.

Across the world, many people know the weight of political turmoil as they are ruled by leaders who choose greed, idolatry, and injustice over caring for God's creation. Yet in the same way God saw Judah's pain, he sees ours, and the hope of the promised Messiah is our hope too. As we celebrate Jesus' first coming, we eagerly await his return. We need "the Lord Our Righteousness" to reign. We need Jesus.

REFLECT

Reflecting on the failures of the human kings in Judah, what does it reveal about the importance of leadership that reflects God's justice and righteousness? In what ways can we apply this principle in our own lives and spheres of influence?

How does the reign of Jesus as the "righteous Branch" bring about the restoration of shalom and the defeat of sin?

READ
ISAIAH 7:10-14

A Relentless Love

WHEN WE ARE AFRAID, GOD PURSUES OUR HEARTS

BY ALEXANDRA HOOVER

I remind my young son every day how much I love him. Over the past months, I'd noticed he'd been worried and sad. Like many kids his age, he was weighed down by the news of school shootings, riots, a pandemic, and political tensions. If I'm being honest, I was also deeply afraid. But I reminded my son often, "Kingston, you are so loved. We are safe. God is with us in this—even if you can't feel it." My son, like many of us, has a difficult time believing this. The world is heavy—where is hope?

In Isaiah 7:10–14, we find a frightened King Ahaz in the midst of impending political danger and strife. Enemies are closing in on the nation of Judah, and the need to look elsewhere for rescue and reprieve has welled up in Ahaz's wayward heart. The king knew God's law, but he didn't trust in it. Where God sought to offer safety, Ahaz was ruled by idolatry, even to the point of sacrificing his son (2 Kings 16). God made it clear what this meant for Judah—if Ahaz didn't listen to his instructions and take heed, destruction was inevitable (Isa. 10–11).

God's relentless pursuit of the king of Judah was not only for Ahaz's repentance but for the sake of his entire people's salvation, just as Jesus' life, death, resurrection, and ascension are for us. Ahaz's eyes were distracted by the temporary, while eternal perspective was knocking at his door. But just as God's grace continues in our unfaithfulness, even in Ahaz's contention and rejection of God's power and presence, Isaiah gives him a sign: "Behold, the virgin shall conceive and bear a son, and shall call his name Immanuel" (Isa. 7:14 , ESV).

A great salvation will arrive through the birth of Jesus. Hope is now here (Matt. 1:20–22). God is with us, in the midst of our turmoil and often treacherous conditions. He has come down to offer eternal hope in our momentary afflictions. He asks us to listen and believe and helps us do this in our weakness and unbelief.

When my son was afraid, I was relentless in the pursuit of his heart, much like God is with ours. I needed my son to know that fear didn't have to rule us but the hope of Christ could. In a season where many of us are tender to the reality of doubt and fear, Jesus' love relentlessly abounds for his people. He is the rescue and the ransom for the lives of many, promising that "as a mother comforts her child, so will I comfort you" (Isa. 66:13). He is our great signpost—a king gifting us life in exchange for his death. Today, don't harden your heart like Ahaz, but instead know that God's power is in you, his presence is with you, and his promise is over you.

REFLECT

- How does the story of King Ahaz demonstrate God's relentless pursuit of his people's hearts and his desire for their salvation?
- In what ways can we find hope and comfort in the assurance that God is with us, even in the midst of fear and turmoil?

READ
LUKE 2:22-32

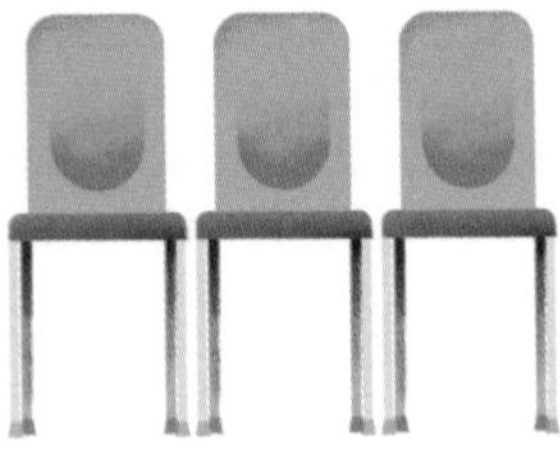

An Unscheduled Appointment

WHAT SIMEON'S LONG-AWAITED ASSURANCE MEANS FOR US TODAY

BY MONTY WALDRON

When was your last waiting-room experience? Mine was a couple weeks ago at the doctor's office. The space was bright, warm, and comfortable. After checking in, one could read from the stack of magazines, catch a show on the flatscreen, scroll through socials, or just stare out the window to pass the time. But the waiting was compulsory. No one in the room got around it, and the delay was almost certainly longer than any of us would have liked. There's something in us that wants life to happen according to schedule—our schedule. Often, our waiting is linked to an appointment that we've made. We've agreed to see so-and-so for such-and-such at an agreed-upon time. But if that time passes, we wait, and the longer the wait, the more agitated we become.

What if you knew you had an appointment of sorts with the most powerful person in the universe, but it wasn't set on a calendar? What if you were told that you would have an audience with the King of Kings but given no date or time—told only that it would be sometime before you die? That's what happened to Simeon.

"Now there was a man in Jerusalem called Simeon, who was righteous and devout. He was waiting for the consolation of Israel, and the Holy Spirit was on him. It had been revealed to him by the Holy Spirit that he would not die before he had seen the Lord's Messiah" (Luke 2:25–26).

How's that for a waiting-room experience? Imagine waking up every day wondering, *Will it be today?* No doubt the promise revealed by the Holy Spirit was memorable and compelling. But surely there were moments when Simeon felt the weight of waiting for the one and only, the singular source of salvation for humanity. How did he persevere through the agitation that comes with knowing the end of the story but having to live with the uncertainty of the in-between? I can only conclude that Simeon's devotion was rooted in the person with the plan, more than the plan itself. Perhaps he didn't presume to have an opinion on the timetable or particulars— maybe he was able to treat them as the domain of divine sovereignty. Simeon was joyfully content to see it all unfold before his eyes, confident that the one who promised would do just as he said, at the perfect time, and for the good of all who "have longed for his appearing" (2 Tim. 4:8).

What a gift it is in this season to see the arrival of God's salvation through Simeon's eyes. I want to wait well, as he did, full of assurance that the King will return just as he promised. He keeps his appointments. And on that day, we will depart in peace, joining a great cloud of witnesses, face-to-face with our salvation (Rev. 22:1–5).

REFLECT

We're invited to consider a different kind of waiting—the anticipation of an audience with the King of Kings. How does this shift in perspective deepen your understanding of waiting on God's timing and his promises in your life?

Simeon's devotion was rooted in the person with the plan rather than focusing solely on the plan itself. How can you apply this principle to your own life? How does trusting in God's sovereignty give you confidence?

READ
LUKE 4:16-21

The Synagogue Visit That Changed Everything

HOW JESUS' ARRIVAL RELIEVES OUR ANXIOUS WAITING

BY KRISTEL ACEVEDO

Not long ago, a friend of mine took my daughter to the mall with her family. I was grateful for a morning of uninterrupted work and was about to go pick her up when I heard my husband's phone ring. It was my friend's husband: "There was a shooting at the mall. I talked to my wife—she and the girls are okay, but they're being held on the premises and haven't been allowed to leave yet."

I got to the mall in record time and, dizzy with urgency, did the hardest waiting of my life. Waiting for updates from the police; waiting to be able to speak with my friend to find out what happened. Waiting to hold my daughter in my arms; waiting to inspect her injuries; waiting to ease her fears and mine.

Urgent fear resonates through so much around us, whether directly, in the lives of those we love, or the stream of information on wars, disease, corruption, and violence. The need is urgent—where is our hope? As I struggle to keep hopelessness at bay, I imagine how the ancient Jewish community might have felt as they awaited their deliverance and the arrival of the Messiah. It had been 400 years since they had heard from God, and they were subject to overwhelming oppression and crushing captivity. They must have wondered if God had forgotten them and whether a Savior was truly coming.

And then one day, a man named Jesus walked into the synagogue and stood up to read from the scroll of the prophet Isaiah:

> The Spirit of the Lord is on me,
> because he has anointed me
> to preach good news to the poor.
> He has sent me
> to proclaim release to the captives
> and recovery of sight to the blind,
> to set free the oppressed,
> to proclaim the year of the Lord's favor.
> (Luke 4:18–19, CSB)

Jesus wasn't finished yet, though. He wasn't simply reminding them of a future they could look forward to. Instead, he made an astounding proclamation that would have made jaws drop: "Today as you listen, this Scripture has been fulfilled" (v. 21).

It's the official announcement from Jesus that he is ushering in the kingdom of God. As we follow him, we no longer walk through the bad news of our world with despair. Instead, we look to Jesus sitting on his throne. We can stand on his promise of redemption, even when we face horrifying circumstances in our own lives, like the day I waited for my daughter at the mall. When I finally saw her face and held her body to mine, the relief and joy I felt was unlike any I have experienced before. It was a reminder to me that God is not done. That this is not the end. The King is here, and eternal jubilee is at hand.

REFLECT

- How does the author's story of urgency and fearfulness resonate with your own experiences of waiting and longing for deliverance or hope in difficult situations?

- When Jesus proclaimed the fulfillment of the messianic mandate from Isaiah, he declared that the kingdom of God had arrived. As followers of Jesus, how does this proclamation empower us to approach the challenges and darkness of our world with hope and action?

READ
ISAIAH 35:4-10

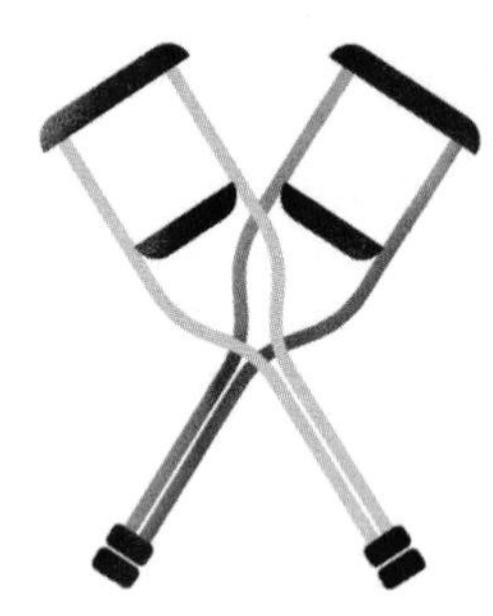

He Is Not One to Leave Us Hurting

THE DIFFICULT WORK OF EMBODIED FAITH

BY BECA BRUDER

It's not easy to both inhabit our bodies and trust in the work of the Spirit. Illness, disability, and abuse are part of our reality and urgently grip our focus. Our minds are often filled with dizzying, self-obsessed thoughts, and our own woes monopolize our attention.

We want relief: a place for our parched souls to find water, where the limitations of our bodies can be overcome. We cry out for rescue and vengeance for the injustices our bodies have absorbed. We hope to see Christ in the bubbling springs but get distracted by the burning sand underneath our feet.

The prophet Isaiah revealed God's promise in the language of healing. Yes, the Messiah will bring spiritual peace, but he will not overlook the wounded bodies of the redeemed. He will usher us into Zion with singing and lead us to the bright dawning of our hope. He is not one to leave us hurting.

Though we know the promise, we're prone to wander, following our own paths of disbelief. Christ's redemption often takes a different shape than we imagined it would, and we, like John the Baptist, wonder if we are to wait for another king. Did we entrust our hope to the wrong person? Is he not who we thought he was? We long for our rescue to come and for it to tangibly change our reality. Jesus' reply to John's question is on those terms: "The blind receive sight, the lame walk, those who have leprosy are cleansed, the deaf hear, the dead are raised, and the good news is proclaimed to the poor" (Matt. 11:4–5).

He is the salvation Isaiah prophesied. The healing that comes from his hand testifies to his divinity. Israel waited for the coming of a Savior who would heal both spiritual and physical brokenness. That hope became reality in a baby's birth. His miracles during his time on earth were the first signs of that long-expected healing. And yet, we still wait for him, torn and fragile.

Instead of letting our debilitation discourage devotion, we lift expectant eyes to the one who can save. This season, we will echo the hopes of ancient Israel as we sing, "O come, O come, Emmanuel." There will be a time when the entirety of this prophecy will be our reality. We will walk in the holy way with the redeemed. Everlasting joy and gladness will be upon our heads and all sorrow will flee.

Until then, we remember the baby born in Bethlehem who came to open the eyes of the blind and proclaim good news to the poor and who will return to gather and save God's people. He will bring divine retribution for the wrongs and healing for our hurts, and we will be made whole. "Say to those with fearful hearts, 'Be strong, do not fear; your God will come' " (Isa. 35:4).

REFLECT

As we reflect on the prophetic words of Isaiah and the healing ministry of Jesus, how does this bring comfort and hope to our own struggles with physical limitations, illnesses, or injustices?

How can we encourage one another to remain steadfast and strong in faith, despite the trials and challenges we face?

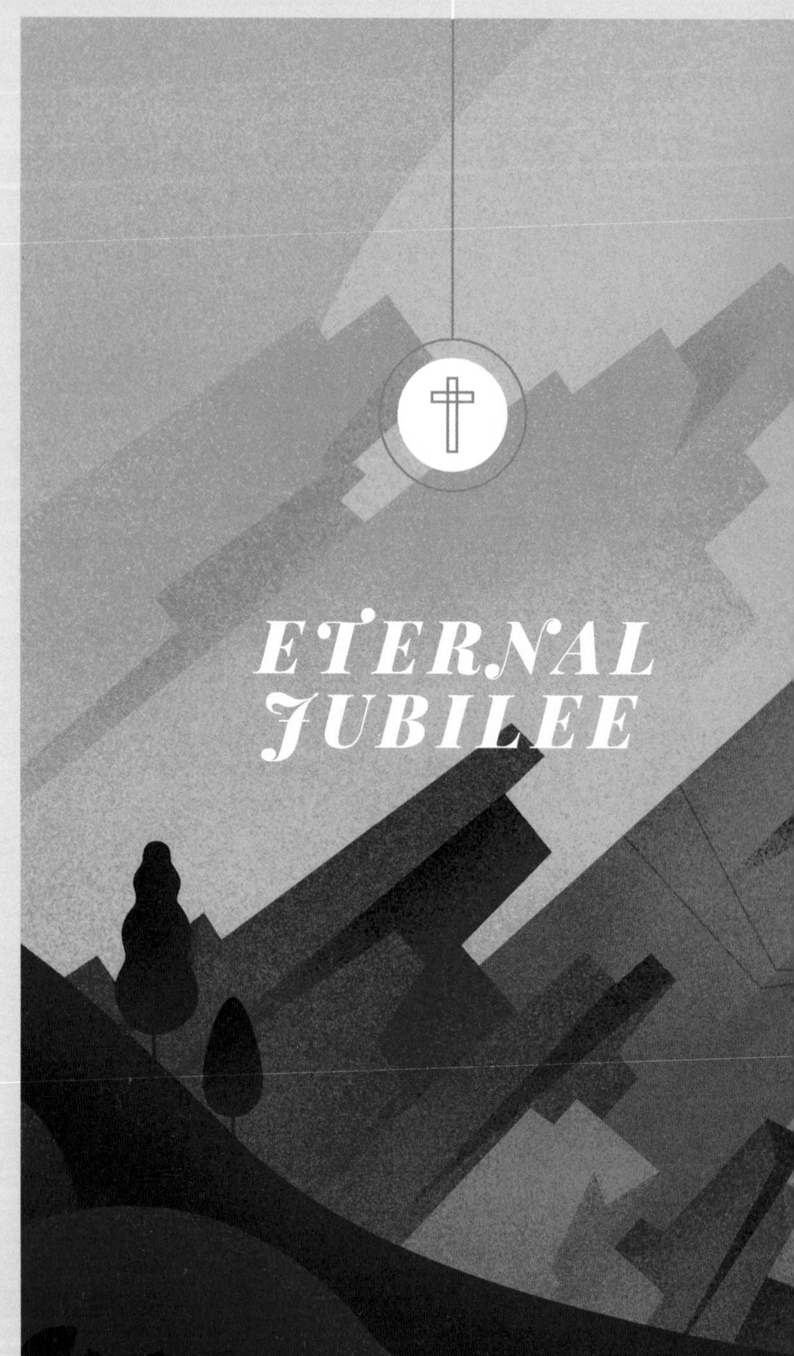
ETERNAL
JUBILEE

READ
JOHN 16:33

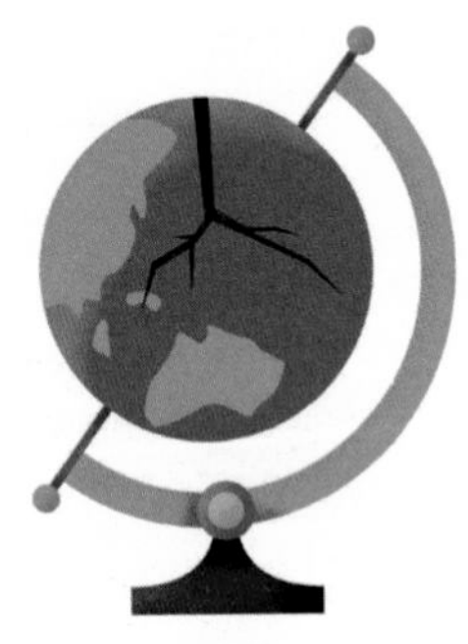

The Good News About Our Bad News

SOMETIMES, SUFFERING CAN'T BE SPIRITUALIZED

BY STRAHAN COLEMAN

I have some good news for you: There's going to be bad news.

Christ's incarnation was punctuated by bad news. His arrival saw the slaughter of a generation at the hands of a tyrant. His ministry climaxed with his torture and execution. Even after the victory of the Resurrection and birth of the church at Pentecost, his Spirit-filled followers were persecuted and exiled, "scattered throughout the provinces of Pontus, Galatia, Cappadocia, Asia, and Bithynia" (1 Pet. 1:1). Eventually the church took the gospel global, only to suffer pain and division over petty theological disagreements and cults of personality. I imagine this is not the messianic story Israel had expected, nor was it the dream of the early church.

We live in a culture obsessed with eradicating pain—inventing and selling technologies to insulate against it, pills to dull it, or self-help techniques to avoid it. It's unpopular to say "Life is hard; expect to suffer," but it's true.

Jesus says directly that "in this world you will have trouble" (John 16:33), and though we have heard this, many of us have found ourselves shocked, angry, and unprepared when we actually *do* experience deep suffering. As the dust settles, we realize our reactions to life's troubles don't match the theological truths we affirm.

I've been jarred by this dissonance more than a few times. Jesus' teaching that we can expect a life filled with bad news—and expect him to lead us through it—is actually very good news.

Knowing that suffering is coming inoculates us from a shallow spirituality that believes pain can be avoided or attributes difficulties to unfaithfulness. It is no exception or failing when we suffer—it's a baked-in fact of life. If we believe that our efforts or positive thinking will protect us from pain, we are set up for existential shock when it comes. Christ is forthright about this reality and invites us to accept both the inevitability of trouble and the assurance that he has overcome it. This reality is actually quite liberating.

Christ overcame the world's suffering and temptations in the same way that he overcame death: not by removing it but by traveling through it faithfully, allowing it to become the very vehicle by which he offers salvation to the whole cosmos. In John 16, Jesus invites us to do the same by living from the peace of his Spirit rather than the anxiety of our circumstance, seeing the trouble of the world as an aberration held in Christ's hands, an expected reality we are empowered to walk through.

Suffering will come, and sometimes it will be the sort you can't spiritualize and probably think you can't face. When it happens, don't be surprised, and don't think it's on you to make it into a miracle. Remember that it is Christ who overcomes—trust him, lean in, and allow him to do the work of saving you and the world through it. This is the earthy reality of the Advent story. Hallelujah!

REFLECT

How do you personally respond to suffering and difficult circumstances?

How can you lean on Christ's example and the peace of his Spirit during times of suffering?

READ
JOHN 3:16-21

A Universe-Sized Love

THE THRILL OF HOPE THAT EMERGES IN OUR HEARTS AT ADVENT

BY RONNIE MARTIN

I love the interplay between Nicodemus and Jesus in the Gospel of John. He meets Jesus at night to avoid judgment from his fellow Pharisees because he wants time to ask Jesus some honest questions. The keeper of the Jewish customs wants to get to the bottom of what's intriguing him about this man who speaks with such authority.

Jesus responds so patiently and kindly to Nicodemus's candor. He communicates his mission to the world by framing it in love, which is interesting when you consider that Nicodemus was a teacher of the law. In his kindness, Jesus shows Nicodemus that in God's universe-sized love, he gave his only Son so that whoever believes will not be condemned to an eternity without God.

What kind of love is Jesus talking about here? I know that I use the word *love* a little generically in order to show my affection for something: I love this kind of food, I love my job, I love this TV show, I love my hobby. This is a kind of love.

But through Jesus, God revealed the kind of love he has for us and what effect he intended that love to have on us: "See what great love the Father has lavished on us, that we should be called children of God! And that is what we are!" (1 John 3:1).

Jesus' big reveal about the design and depth of God's love is calling us children of God. But it's a love that came at a massive cost, which always comes with the greatest kind of love. "Greater love has no one than this: to lay down one's life for one's friends," Jesus says in John 15:13. This wasn't merely an affection, a squishy feeling, or a special fondness for us. The love of God for us goes even deeper and wider than the universe itself, because "God is love. Whoever lives in love lives in God, and God in them," John tells us in 1 John 4:16.

Though we are born in a darkness that comprises the depths of our souls, God sent Jesus to burst through the blackness with a light that is bright enough to illuminate the farthest reaches of the universe. Jesus didn't merely lay out the blueprints for God's redemption; he also included God's motivation: love. This is the thrill of hope that reemerges in our hearts every year at Advent, as we imagine the unfathomable volume of God's love for us in the person and work of Jesus Christ.

REFLECT

Nicodemus, a teacher of the law, seeks answers from Jesus and encounters the profound message of God's love. How does Jesus' framing of his mission in terms of love challenge our understanding of the common cultural notions of love?

Advent is a season of anticipating and celebrating the unfathomable volume of God's love manifested in Jesus Christ. How can we cultivate a sense of awe and gratitude for the immeasurable love of God in our lives?

READ
2 CORINTHIANS 3:17-18

How to Behold the Glory

WE ARE CONTINUALLY BECOMING WHAT WE BEHOLD

BY STEVE WOODROW

The first time the word *glory* really captured my attention was on a hot Sunday morning at a predominantly Black church in Atlanta, Georgia. I was the young guest preacher, and "Glory!" rose up repeatedly from the back row of pews as I spoke, rich in cadence and with undeniable spiritual authority. The bold group of women in the back were in tune with something that I, as a fresh graduate from seminary, was not. As I spoke to their beloved church, I was more focused on intellectually connecting the dots of my text and passing along my knowledge of the Scriptures than in the reality of this glory they so beautifully proclaimed. For me at the time, the word *glory* did not occupy much space in my thoughts or conversation. The concept seemed vague and even made me a bit uncomfortable. But that day, I decided I needed to know what those women knew. I spoke with them after the service, and it was abundantly clear that they were not shouting rote religious words to stir up emotion—they had been experiencing the gathering of the saints and the preaching of the Word as a sharing in his glory and as fellowship with the Holy Spirit.

Their vibrant faith reminded me that we are becoming what we behold. As we fix our eyes on Jesus and experience the presence and power of God in our lives, we understand and reflect glory more and more. On the other hand, the greatest bondage comes when we fix our eyes on ourselves or the idols that surround us. Jesus made a way for the Spirit's indwelling, so that we could be set free from bondage to sin and behold the Lord's glory. His advent removes the veil over our hearts and offers both the blessing of beholding his glory and that of being transformed into the same glory (2 Cor. 3:17–18).

On that Sunday morning many years ago, it was clear to me—and those around me—that I was out of my comfort zone. As I expressed my own challenges after the service, one woman declared, "He'll get you through!" I have needed that encouragement to fix my eyes on Jesus throughout the journey of life and my pastoral vocation. Those women were, for me, like the angels who proclaimed "Glory to God in the highest heaven" (Luke 2:13–14), declaring the glory of the Lord and pointing me to the presence, power, and peace of my Savior. I wish they were part of my church every Sunday, helping me behold Jesus, who came so that we could all become like him.

REFLECT

Considering the significance of the word *glory* in the context of a worship service, how would you describe your understanding of glory? How has this concept influenced your relationship with God and your worship?

We often express gratitude for the impact of church community in helping us behold Jesus. In what ways does your faith community support and encourage you in your journey of beholding God's glory?

READ
1 PETER 2:9

We Forget We Belong to God

THE HEALING BALM OF FINDING OUR TRUE IDENTITY

BY ELIZABETH WOODSON

To celebrate the eternal king's inauguration is to celebrate how, through Jesus, we find freedom from the bondage of sin and death. We who were far off have been brought near into a restored relationship and eternal rest with God (Eph. 2:13).

Peter's words were written to Gentile Christians living as "foreigners and exiles" in the Roman Empire (1 Pet. 2:11). They were noncitizens or temporary residents in a world that highly valued citizenship in its social hierarchy. It was also a time when Rome's tolerance for religious freedom was diminishing. Peter was writing to marginalized and persecuted Christians, suffering for their allegiance to King Jesus. In 1 Peter 2:9, the apostle provides his readers with a healing balm, a reminder that God, not people, determined their true identity. Peter uses four phrases to describe their identity in Christ: a chosen people, a royal priesthood, a holy nation, and God's special possession.

His words point back to Exodus 19:4–6, where God explained to Moses the purpose behind his desired covenant with Israel. Israel had been set apart to show the world what it meant to worship the one true God. They would experience his blessing as they served as a conduit for God's blessing to the world.

Suffering and persecution can dehumanize and demoralize a people, stripping them of their dignity and hope. What the world tried to take from these Christians, Peter sought to restore. He reminded these "foreigners and exiles" of their elevated status. Through Christ, they were members of the family of Abraham with direct access to the divine. They had an eternal status as royal priests set apart to lead the nations to God.

Through the gospel, we who have been dehumanized are rehumanized, clothed with strength and dignity because of the one in whose image we are made.

But in a world infected with sin and evil, it can be easy to forget.

We forget we belong to God. Blinded by the struggles of life, we have difficulty seeing the eternal hope we have simply because we are his.

But in the words of Shirley Caesar, "This hope that we have, the world didn't give it to us, and the world can't take it away." No matter how dark the night is, we always have hope. Through Christ, God's steadfast love and faithfulness follow us forever. So, in the midst of suffering and persecution, our eyes look to the eternal, not the temporal. We remember that our identity, value, and calling are determined by God, not by man. We will be his people for eternity; our forever home is with him.

REFLECT

How does understanding our identity as a chosen people and God's special possession shape our perspective on suffering and persecution?

In what ways does the world try to define our identity and value? How can we guard against forgetting that our true identity is determined by God?

READ
JOHN 3:25-30

The Goodness of Growing Smaller

HOW TO TRUST GOD IN A SEASON OF DECREASE

BY LAURA WIFLER

It is never fun to feel as though you've been replaced, and John the Baptist's disciples really didn't like it. As John and his followers were baptizing near Salim, Jesus also began baptizing in the Judean countryside nearby. Alarmed that this new teacher was enjoying more success than their own, John's disciples voiced worry to John that "everyone" was going to Jesus to be baptized (John 3:26, CSB throughout), perhaps expecting similar indignation or a competitive response from their teacher. John instead showed them the beauty of gospel paradox.

His disciples feared the unexpected turn of events, but John reminds his followers of what he'd been saying all along: "I am not the Messiah, but I've been sent ahead of him" (v. 28). In fact, upon hearing the news of Jesus' success, John says his joy "is complete" (v. 29). John's popularity was ending. His success fading. His influence declining. For most of us, this would be cause for discouragement and envy, yet for John, it brought joy. This is the beautiful paradox of the gospel. The Christian life is about losing to find. Giving to gain. Dying to live. That means sometimes growing smaller, losing outward influence, or lessening in rank is a good thing.

John says, "He must increase, but I must decrease" (v. 30). In a season typically associated with busyness and increase—more things to do, more things to buy, and more people to see—maybe you are in a season of decrease. You may have lost a loved one and find fewer chairs at the table. Having lost a job, your calendar may be emptier and the pile of gifts around your tree may be smaller. Much like John's disciples, we may worry or mourn the changes. Yet just before reminding his disciples that he is not the Messiah, John reminds them that everything is a gift from God (v. 27). You see, John had a proper view of his assignment. He didn't think of himself too highly, as if he were Christ himself, but he also knew he had value and purpose in God's plan. In John 1, the author reminds the reader that John "was not the light, but he came to testify about the light" (v. 8). Christ is the "true light" (v. 9). John knew his role was important, but it wasn't the ultimate point.

During this Advent season, we can embrace the fact that any success we have is not of our own doing but is heaven's goodness undeservedly poured out on our lives. We can defer to what God has for us, whether he gives or takes away, because our lives are not our own but belong to God (1 Cor. 6:19). No matter where we are in life, we can humbly trust the plans of the true light, and bear witness to his fame.

REFLECT

- In what ways can we find joy and purpose in seasons of decrease or diminishing influence?
- How does the reminder that all our gifts and successes are from God shape our perspective during the Advent season and encourage us to humbly trust his plans?

READ
EPHESIANS 1:15-23

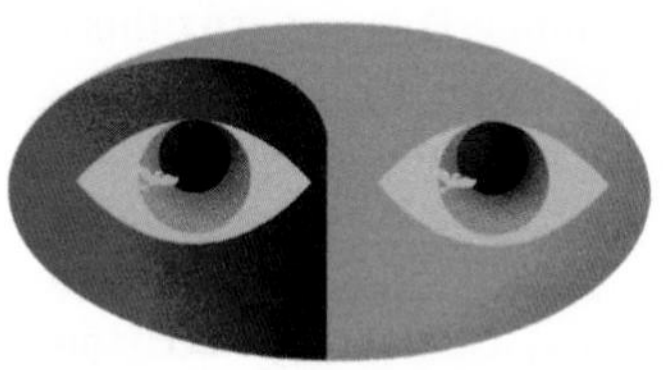

True Hope Cannot Be Manufactured

WHAT HAPPENS WHEN WE EMBRACE THE LIMITS OF OUR STRENGTH?

BY CARLOS WHITTAKER

A hard truth—the kind that makes us wince—might not be the best way to start off a Christmas devotional, but just hang with me as I explain: Hope takes a lot of work. Yes, Jesus brings us ultimate hope, but like many aspects of Christian faith, living with hope doesn't always come easily. The story of our faith might include some scenic sunny days on the Sea of Galilee, but it is based on a cross. We know, if we're honest, that the journey is not going to be easy, so let's digest some truths that can nourish us and build up this thing called hope.

In Ephesians 1, Paul writes to the church about the reality of hope and how it isn't tied to anything that the church itself can accomplish. That offers some relief: It isn't about what we can do. No, hope takes the stage when the church stops trying to pull it off themselves and places their hope instead in the power of Christ and his authority over all things.

It sounds simple to just "let go and let God," as the pithy tagline goes, but think again. Try to remember the last time that you had to stop trying to pull things off on your own and allow someone to do it for you—work projects, parenting, or even your own ministry. This level of trust and release of control can feel next to impossible. We love to say that we place our hope in Jesus, but it's so much easier to place our hope in our own skill sets and abilities. That's why hope takes work, because it is work to let go of control.

Realizing the limits of my own strength helps me rely on Jesus to be the author of hope in my life. In Ephesians 1:19, Paul speaks of the immeasurable greatness of God's power. In comical contrast, I wake up each morning in my 49-year-old body and I limp. Sleep is now apparently a contact sport, and when I go to the gym, my goal is to stretch enough to not be sore when I get up the next morning. My strength has limits. But Ephesians makes it clear that the strength of the one who *actually* gives us hope is immeasurable. There are no limits to his greatness and power. None. That is truly something we can all place our hope in, no matter the circumstances.

Here's the kicker: The authority of our all-powerful King has actually been bestowed on us out of the riches of his grace, and it lives inside us as Christians. We can tap into the authority of our creator this Christmas season to allow his strength to flow in and through us. In the midst of all the hubbub of the season, with the inevitable weary minds and sore bodies, allow your hope to be found in his strength and authority. It's better that way.

REFLECT

Reflecting on the concept of hope, how does the realization that hope requires letting go of control resonate with your own journey of faith? In what areas of your life do you find it challenging to surrender control and trust in God's power?

As Christians, we have access to the authority of our all-powerful King. In what ways can you tap into his strength and authority during the Christmas season, amid the busyness and weariness?

DIVINE CORONATION

READ
COLOSSIANS 1:15-20

Flutters of the Firstborn of Creation

HOW WE LOVE EVEN WHAT WE DON'T YET SEE

BY CAROLINE GREB

At this time of year, we are bombarded with images that nag at our attention, presenting us with the idea of the perfectly peaceful holiday and all the gifts that will truly satisfy us. Imagine, for a minute, loving something you've never seen. Even without fully understanding what you are loving, there is an ache and a hope for fulfillment, for completion, for wholeness. But what about loving some*one* you've never seen?

This is a concept mothers know well, feeling their babies move in the womb before ever seeing their faces. Perhaps this is what Mary felt for nine long months as her stomach grew, trying to make sense of the fact that the little flutters and punches were the first movements of the Son of the Most High.

For 2,000 years, God had revealed his presence in the various forms of smoke, fire, manna-giver, and cloud on a mountaintop. It was impossible—and forbidden—to attempt any picture or representation of him. He was invisible, unable to be whittled down to an image and unable to be comprehended by our human eyes.

True worship always holds God's immanence and his transcendence in tension. Where can we conceive of that worship more than in his enfleshing, his incarnation? God in his grace made the invisible visible and chose to dwell among his people as one of us. But not only did the firstborn of the dead come in our fragile human form; he came as the weakest of us all—a newborn. God became a helpless creature in need of the most basic human requirements: being fed, clothed, and kept clean. It's difficult to even imagine the fullness of God somehow fitting into a six-pound newborn. This infant was the mover at the beginning of creation, present before time began and preeminent in all things. In him—the babe who couldn't hold his own head up—all things hold together. Jesus in the manger is an image we may not expect, but the God of humility, servanthood, and reconciliation is the one that we need.

But the story unfolds further; the image becomes clearer. In a feeble, tiny body, God was pleased to dwell. It was not his obligation or an inconvenience to reveal himself to us this way, but his pure pleasure. And even now, it continues to be God's pure pleasure—his joy—to reveal himself, to give of himself even when he doesn't need to, to rule as a humble King, for our good and our joy. It is his delight to bring reconciliation, to restore the very creation he made in its edenic beginning and, yes, to lift the veil and make a way for us to see him face to face.

He is the image of the God we need—a God who exemplifies humility, servanthood, and pleasure in reconciliation. He holds all things together, from creation to the manger to the cross to the new creation.

REFLECT

Considering the analogy of a mother feeling her baby's movements in the womb, how does it deepen your understanding of Mary's experience and the significance of Jesus' incarnation?

Contemplating the tension between God's immanence and transcendence, as exemplified in Jesus' incarnation, how does the image of a helpless newborn challenge our notions of power and greatness?

READ
LUKE 1:26-38

The Suspense of Mary's Yes

HOW A COURAGEOUS RESPONSE ECHOES THROUGH ETERNITY

BY MALCOLM GUITE

In Luke chapter 1, we are presented with a beautiful account of how the angel came to Mary, how she heard him, and how she responded in courage: "I am the Lord's servant. May your word to me be fulfilled." The words contained here should fill every faithful reader with awe and wonder, but above all with gratitude. These few verses in Luke are one of the great hinges—or momentous turning points—of the whole Bible. They are an answer to that early tragic turning point in Genesis: the moment of Eve's disobedience.

Eve's choice had terrible consequences for all of us. Her yes to the serpent foreclosed and diminished our true humanity—though of course, the serpent had promised just the opposite! But if Eve turned her back on God, and turned all of us with her, then Mary turns to face him willingly, and her courageous yes to God welcomes Jesus into the world. In Jesus every person may now choose, if they wish, to receive God's welcome. His welcome extends both to the fullness of life here on earth, even with all its limitations, and into eternal life with him.

Our God is the God of freedom and love, and he will not force himself on anyone. Instead, he waits courteously for our assent, for our yes to his love. As we read these verses, we almost hold our breaths and reenter the drama of that moment: God offers to come into the world as our savior, and Mary, at this moment, speaks for all of us. What will she say? Will she offer her whole life to be made new, to be changed forever? Or will she shy away from the burden?

We should sense an awesome hush, an agony of suspense, between verses 37 and 38, and then as we hear Mary's response, we should feel great relief and rejoicing. Mary's yes not only changes everything forever but also models for us our own Christian life. Now we too are called not to be afraid but to be open, to say to God, *I too am your servant. Let your word to me be fulfilled.* In the sonnet below, I have tried to evoke a little of the suspense and importance of this moment.

We see so little, stayed on surfaces,
We calculate the outsides of all things,
Preoccupied with our own purposes
We miss the shimmer of the angels' wings,
They coruscate around us in their joy
A swirl of wheels and eyes and wings unfurled,
They guard the good we purpose to destroy,
A hidden blaze of glory in God's world.
But on this day a young girl stopped to see
With open eyes and heart. She heard the voice;
The promise of His glory yet to be,
As time stood still for her to make a choice;
Gabriel knelt and not a feather stirred,
The Word himself was waiting on her word.

This sonnet, "Annunciation," is from *Sounding the Seasons* (Canterbury Press, 2012) and is used with the author's permission.

REFLECT

Reflecting on Mary's response to the angel's message, how does her courageous yes to God's plan inspire and challenge you in your own journey of faith?

In what ways, like Mary, can you cultivate a spirit of openness and surrender?

READ
MATTHEW 1:18-25

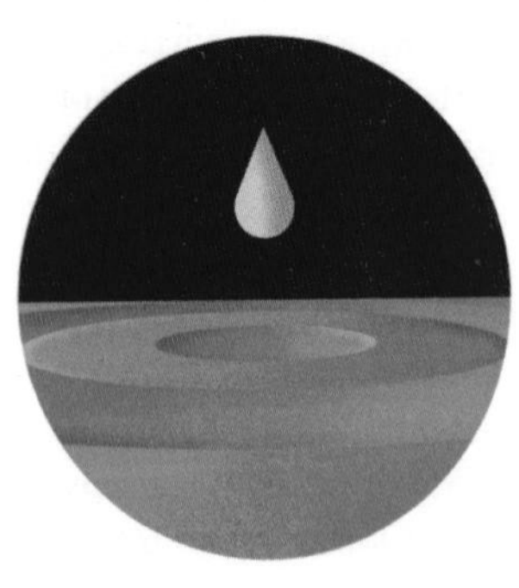

Why Joseph Is Known as the Silent Saint

HOW TO LISTEN FOR GOD'S LEADING WHEN THINGS SEEM TO GO WRONG

BY JOY CLARKSON

Joseph is known as the silent saint. Though his part in the story of Christ is not small—his is the royal line Jesus claims, his the profession Jesus adopts—he does not say a single word in any of the Gospels. This is something of a theme in the stories surrounding Jesus' birth: Zechariah struck silent in the temple and Joseph quietly considering how to proceed, while Mary and Elizabeth burst forth in prophetic utterance, early proclamations of the gospel.

But just because Joseph does not speak should not lead us to think that he is passive. Indeed, Joseph is presented to us as a man of decisive action emerging from a rich inner life. We are told that upon learning his wife-to-be is pregnant, he does not immediately break their engagement, subjecting her to public embarrassment and possibly much worse. Despite what any wounded fiancé in the fresh pain of apparent unfaithfulness might be tempted to do, Joseph instead forms a merciful and wise plan.

The only character description we are given of Joseph is that he is "faithful to the law" (v. 19). So, without publicizing Mary's situation to anyone (as far as we are told), he decides on a plan that is both faithful to the law and gracious to Mary. All this he comes to privately, and we can only assume painfully, and all his pain and his generosity remain beneath the surface. The silent saint has a virtue that simmers beneath the surface, where his self-control in the face of being wronged restrains him and allows him not only to forbear but also protect Mary, the source of his pain.

And as with many people who have made fraught decisions within themselves, something bubbles up for Joseph from even deeper beneath the surface: a dream, and with it an angel. This dream must have come as a comfort, an assurance, and with a good deal of confusion. All this is not recorded. Only that Joseph, who was faithful to the law, the Word of the Lord, was faithful to this word from the angel. Within himself once again he resolves to act, without any outpouring of prophetic speech. He let people think that he, a thoughtful and self-controlled man, had gotten her pregnant with child in a moment of lapsed self-control. He took Mary's shame onto himself, perhaps foreshadowing what Jesus would do for all humankind. And all this he did without saying a word.

Ours is a world drowning in words. In Joseph, the silent saint, I see a different way of being—a way of silence and action, where sometimes the most important words are the ones we don't speak.

REFLECT

Reflecting on Joseph's silent but decisive actions, what can we learn about the power of silent strength and self-control in our own lives? How can we cultivate a similar posture of silence and action in the midst of challenging situations?

Consider the role of dreams and divine guidance in Joseph's story. How can we be attuned to God's voice and guidance in our own lives? How can we discern his will and trust his leading, even when it may be confusing or challenging?

READ
LUKE 1:39-55

The Contrast Between Two Mothers

HOW MARY AND ELIZABETH EXALT GOD THROUGH THEIR MUTUAL JOY

BY DOROTHY BENNETT

Often when we find ourselves in a similar season of life to those around us, we note how they are handling their situation compared to our own. It can be dating in high school, the wedding season that starts in college and continues into the following decade, and especially the era of bearing children. In our lives, competition may be the natural underbelly of this comparison, but in Luke's account, that is thoroughly eclipsed by the focus on God's coming kingdom.

The angel Gabriel announced to Mary that she would miraculously bear a son and that her cousin Elizabeth had also become pregnant in her old age. When Mary visited Elizabeth, surely the two women would have noticed where their situations diverged. Elizabeth's disgrace among her people was taken away in pregnancy; Mary's began in pregnancy. Elizabeth's son was given through the institution of marriage; Mary's was conceived by the Holy Spirit.

The tension I imagine in this meeting is further compounded by the Magnificat. With Christ's imminent entry into the world, Mary's song describes what kind of kingdom he has come to establish. It is one that will reverse societal norms. The proud will be scattered, the rich sent away empty. The humble will be lifted and the hungry filled with good things. It is clear when reading Luke that Elizabeth had been lifted up and that Mary was lifted even higher. To the contemporary, undiscerning eye, however, Elizabeth had a right to be proud and Mary had none.

How understandable it would have been for Mary to only seek shelter in their visit or for Elizabeth to only offer commiseration. Perhaps they could have fallen into the awkwardness of not acknowledging their differences while preparing for the coming births.

But Luke doesn't record tension or sorrow between the two women. He records joy. Beyond the outward manifestation of their pregnancies, the most important similarity between them was the weight of the miraculous—evidence that God is present, active, and deeply invested in us. As Charles Spurgeon said about the Magnificat, "Oh, how we ought to rejoice in him, whatever our union with him may cost us!"

Elizabeth's exultation and Mary's song cause me to ask myself some poignant questions: Do my eyes look for the movements of God even when they go against what is socially acceptable? Would I declare someone blessed even if it required humility in my deepest desires?

Because he is merciful, my soul should glorify and my spirit rejoice. I want to joyfully exclaim in the midst of our differences like Elizabeth or sing praises in the face of communal persecution like Mary—not for the sake of being contrarian but to be focused on the coming glory of Christ's kingdom.

REFLECT

How does the encounter between Mary and Elizabeth challenge our tendency to compare ourselves to others and compete with them?

In what ways do Mary and Elizabeth demonstrate humility and joy in the face of societal expectations and norms?

READ
MATTHEW 2:13-23

From Egypt, Into Eternity

THE PLIGHT OF MARY AND JOSEPH ECHOES THROUGH GENERATIONS

BY KRISTEL ACEVEDO

When my mom was nine months pregnant with me, she and my dad had to flee their country suddenly. A war had broken out and the fighting was spilling out into the streets of the capital where they lived. Because of my dad's line of work, he was targeted by the guerrilla fighters. Our family wasn't safe.

I can picture my mom all those years ago, belly round with innocent life, and I wonder how she felt. I imagine she was fearful, unsure of how the situation would resolve; I imagine my parents feeling lost in the chaos, confused by the way their plans for starting a family had been upended. No one wants to become a refugee at nine months pregnant.

The story contained in Matthew 2:13–23 has become more and more vivid to me over the years as I've come to see its similarities to the story that my family lived through. I can picture Mary, arms wrapped around her baby. I imagine the fear, confusion, and desperation as they wonder about the implications of saying yes to what God had called them to. No one wants to become a refugee with an infant. Matthew reminds us of Hosea 11:1 in the midst of this story, full of profound prophecy: "When Israel was a child, I loved him, and out of Egypt I called my son." Despite the dark and desperate circumstances, God had a perfect plan and a purpose that would not be thwarted. Although fleeing to escape from a murderous dictator may not seem like God's love in action, we see the bigger, foundational plans as they are fulfilled. The experience of Jesus' family fleeing to and then emerging from the land of Egypt is the fulfillment of Israel's same experience in Exodus. Words that once described the experience of God's corporate people now speak of the Messiah, the Son of God.

As I consider the plight of Mary and Joseph, and even my own mom and dad, I'm reminded of the proverb's wisdom: "a person's heart plans his way, but the Lord determines his steps" (Prov. 16:9, CSB). We make plans, we think we know how God will move, but only he truly knows the steps we will take. Sometimes those steps take us to a place that is comforting and familiar, and sometimes those steps take us away from the only home we know into a new land where we will come to know God as our true and only comfort. My parents were able to settle into a new home in a foreign land. They were able to raise their daughters to know and love Jesus. Mary and Joseph were able to raise Jesus himself and join God's story of rescuing his people, fulfilling a long-awaited prophecy and emerging from that faraway land to establish a new, eternal kingdom. During this season, I am once again amazed at the way God has woven the threads of his unfolding plan, generation to generation.

REFLECT

Reflecting on the experiences of Mary and Joseph's journey, how does this deepen your understanding of their fears, uncertainties, and the unexpected paths they had to take?

The fulfillment of the prophecy in Hosea 11:1 through Jesus' flight to and emergence from Egypt highlights God's perfect plan and purpose that cannot be thwarted. How does this give you hope and reassurance in your own life?

READ
ISAIAH 60:1-3

Out of Darkness, Light

THE LIGHT OF THE WORLD CAME TO CONFRONT OUR SIN

BY JON NITTA

At some point in our childhoods, many of us developed an aversion to the dark. I remember lying in my bed as a young boy with the LA Dodgers game playing softly on the radio, my eyes frantically searching the dark closet trying to discern what the moving shadows were and what dangers they posed. Growing up, we often conjure monsters and nightmares to explain our fear—but most of the time, it's the darkness itself that leaves us deeply unsettled. The experience of darkness as a disorienting reality, full of the unknown, seems to be imprinted deeply on each of our souls. In Genesis 1, God separated light from darkness. This was a purposeful, creative act that was, in God's view, good. Yet after Adam and Eve's rebellious decision and the entry of sin into the world, darkness took on a new meaning. It wasn't just "out there." The darkness was in us and pushing close against us. In Jewish writings such as the Babylonian Talmud, darkness is a metaphor for unsettling disorientation, a dread coming over a person. It also means evil and sin that leave a person struggling for direction, identity, and an understanding of what's in store. Similarly, Isaiah 9 uses the compound word *tzalmavet*—"deep darkness"—to describe the shadow of dark death residing in every human heart.

Isaiah 60:1–3 subtly echoes the familiar story in Genesis 1. Once again there is contrast and separation, light and darkness. But in Isaiah's telling, the enveloping darkness will dissipate—not when the Lord, the author of creation, commands it but rather when he arrives in his fullness. Isaiah is prophesying Advent—the coming of the King—who himself is light to all who are in darkness.

This Advent season, Isaiah's words are an invitation to remember the first Advent. How absolutely undramatic, yet how sublime as the Light of the World humbly came as a baby to confront the darkness of sin in all of us. Isaiah's words are a celebration: "Arise, shine, for your light has come" (v. 1). Light illumines our hearts to understand not only the depth of our sin but also the completed saving work of Jesus for us.

Isaiah's bright words remind us of our calling. We can't greedily hoard this light as we await his second Advent. The light is meant to brilliantly emit out of us so that the nations and our neighbors across the street might see Jesus clearly as the Light of the World (John 8:12). When the gospel of Jesus shines in us more deeply, it can only reflect back out of us through the light of worship and the sharing of the Good News.

REFLECT

How does the concept of darkness in both Genesis and Isaiah symbolize more than just the absence of physical light but also the presence of sin and disorientation in our lives?

How can we embrace the message of Isaiah's prophecy during the Advent season and actively reflect the light of Jesus through worship and sharing the Good News with others?

READ
LUKE 2:13-14

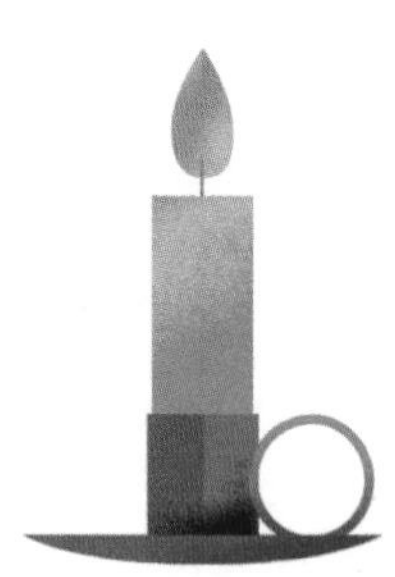

A Symphony of Salvation

AN ANGELIC CELEBRATION THAT IS A FORETASTE OF WHAT'S TO COME

BY ALEXIS RAGAN

In Luke 2:13, we witness a party of angels parading the night sky as they sing a declaration of praise over Christ's arrival on earth as an infant. How marvelous it must have been to hear the shouts of celebration vibrantly filling the air, an honorable demonstration for the divine made flesh. Though we can only imagine what celestial sounds filled the night sky, one familiar piece of music endeavors to offer a glimpse: the famous "Hallelujah Chorus" from Handel's *Messiah*. Here, an angelic choir welcomes Christ's presence and power, accompanied by a symphony that has been treasured for centuries—an earthly rendition of the sound of that sacred evening.

The celebration on that night over 2,000 years ago is a foretaste of what is to come: the celebration that will break out as the Lamb, white as snow, sits at the head of the table, waiting for his bride to arrive. We can see the parallels between the angels' announcement to the shepherds, the soaring music of Handel's *Messiah*, and the "voice of a great multitude" shouting praise over the consummation of Christ and his church in Revelation 19:

> Hallelujah!
> For the Lord our God
> the Almighty reigns.
> Let us rejoice and exult
> and give him the glory,
> for the marriage of the Lamb has come,
> and his Bride has made herself ready;
> it was granted her to clothe herself
> with fine linen, bright and pure.
> (Rev. 19:6-8, ESV)

In this passage, John witnesses the heralding of the ultimate heavenly marriage and the arrival of Christ's bride, who has adorned herself in an array of luminescent garments fit for a celestial ceremony. The intersection of Luke 2 and Revelation 19 renders images of Christ exalted first as a child on earth and then passionately praised and hailed as King of Kings in heaven. Both scenes show the heavenly magnitude by which Christ is recognized as supreme and sovereign, each revealing a heavenly host of worshipers dedicated to giving him glory. In both passages, we recognize the same symphony of salvation that proclaims Jesus' presence and power. As we celebrate Advent, we are invited to make room for a holy observation and take time to contemplate the wonder of his arrival alongside the glory of his eternal reign, participating in the same symphony of salvation.

REFLECT

- How does contemplating these scenes deepen our awe of Christ's coming and his union with his church?
- Reflecting on the parallel between Christ's humble arrival on earth and his glorious reign in heaven, what does this reveal about his divine nature and purpose?

*But the angel said to them,
"Do not be afraid. I bring you
good news that will cause
great joy for all the people.
Today in the town of David a
Savior has been born to you;
he is the Messiah, the Lord."*

LUKE 2:10–11

READ
LUKE 2:8–20

God's Astonishing Announcement Scheme

A DIFFERENT VIEW OF A GLORIOUS ARRIVAL

BY RONNIE MARTIN

The birth of Christ astonishes us.

And not only the birth itself but the way in which God decided to present his Son's birth to the world. With no big-budget marketing plan, social media campaign, or paid TV spots during the Super Bowl, the Lord chose an unsuspecting group of shepherds to introduce *good news of great joy that will be for all people*. Imagine how overwhelmed these poor shepherds must have been as a multitude of otherworldly angels appeared in the dark of night, saying, "Glory to God in the highest, and on earth peace among those with whom he is pleased!" (ESV). We are caught in the throes of wonder when we consider the scale of this spectacle that God arranged for so few people so lacking in cultural influence.

But then we remember Mary, Joseph, a manger, and some animals. A scene that would make most parents shudder if they had to contemplate a birth this simple and obscure. As we grasp to envision these things, we remember that God's idea of his Son's divine childbirth did not include the extravagance and excess that we insist on to illustrate influence and importance.

In God's transcendent economy, lowliness is how he wants us to understand godliness, to understand his Son. As Philippians describes, "Though he was in the form of God, [he] did not count equality with God a thing to be grasped, but emptied himself, by taking the form of a servant" (2:6–7, ESV).

God's astonishing announcement scheme will not likely be featured in leadership books, strategic seminars, or influencer videos for how to boost your brand, gain more followers, and advance your platform. God does something far more bewildering. He sanctifies our comprehension and unravels our values in a very particular way, so that our hearts beat with a pulse that is continuously less in sync with the rhythms of the world. He shares an origin story of peculiar happenings like this, so that thousands of years later, we might treasure and ponder like Mary and return like these shepherds, glorifying and praising God for all we have seen and heard.

Will you lower yourself like Jesus? Will you be led like these shepherds? Will you stop seeing your life as a series of random, dumb-luck circumstances and open your eyes to the astonishing ways God is moving in the ordinary moments of your life? Look around, because the glory of the Lord is shining upon you to fill you with great fear, so that you may experience his great peace.

REFLECT

- The birth of Jesus was announced to a group of shepherds, a marginalized and unlikely audience. How does this unconventional announcement scheme challenge our societal notions of importance, influence, and power?

- The announcement of Jesus' birth challenges our perception of success and the ways in which we often seek recognition and influence in the world. How can we shift our perspective to recognize and appreciate the ordinary moments of our lives as opportunities for God to work and reveal his glory?

READ
ISAIAH 9:2-7

There Is a Light That Changes Everything

THE REAL GIFT OF CHRISTMAS

BY TRILLIA NEWBELL

The Christmas season is upon us! For my kids, this means the anticipation of gifts. I think they begin making their lists on December 26 for the following year. They look forward to and talk about their coming gifts for months and months.

When the gifts finally arrive, they are met with various reactions—some more excited than others. But the one thing that never fails is this: After about an hour, my kids are off doing something completely not related to the very gifts they'd been anticipating all year long. Earthly gifts, though wonderful, aren't ultimately satisfying. They leave us wanting. But there is one gift that is truly satisfying. One gift that keeps on giving. One gift that will never disappoint us, will sustain us, and is always available to us. That gift is Jesus, the Light of the World.

Isaiah prophesies of a baby who will save the world. This surprising announcement came to a rebellious people in a dark time. There was war and unrest. There was no peace to be found. The darkness was palpable, and it went beyond even the circumstances Israel found themselves in. The darkness they experienced was also spiritual; it's a darkness we all experience before we know the Savior.

Jesus fulfills the Old Testament promises of the coming light from Isaiah 9:2: "The people walking in darkness have seen a great light; on those living in the land of deep darkness a light has dawned."

This was a promise of good news to Israel, as it is to us today. The Light of the World has come, and if we follow him, we will also walk in the light—we will have the light of life (1 John 1:7; John 8:12). We don't have to fear destruction because we have been given the light and truth and will no longer walk in darkness. We can be honest and vulnerable. There's no need to hide from Jesus—we couldn't if we tried—for he has come to bring us light and joy. Isaiah's prophecy goes beyond light to victory. There will be glorious life, joy, and victory for God's people (Isa. 9:3–5). And we receive all of this because "to us a child is born, to us a son is given" (v. 6).

The problems of ancient Israel are the same problems we have today: rebellion, war, anger, and strife. The darkness is the same. And if we understand this, it makes the gift and beauty of the light so much brighter.

We all need the hope of Christmas—the hope of a baby born to bring great light. We all need Jesus as much as ancient Israel did, as much as all of humankind does. Equally. Every single one of us. You and I need Jesus, today, tomorrow, and forevermore. Today, we can enjoy him and live with him in the light.

REFLECT

Earthly gifts can leave us unsatisfied and wanting more, but how have you experienced the satisfaction and fulfillment that comes from knowing Jesus?

How can you actively embrace the hope of Christmas and the presence of Jesus in your daily life?

READ
MATTHEW 2:1-12

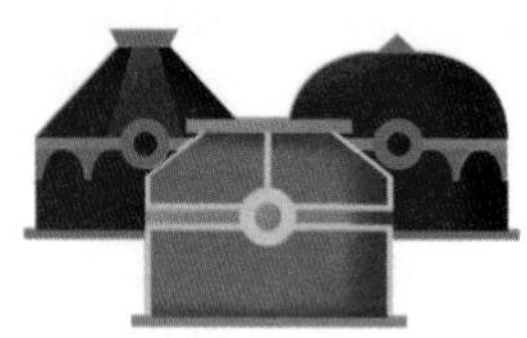

What Made This 'Epiphany' Stand Out?

THE UNIQUE REVELATION OF ADVENT FOR ALL PEOPLE

BY MALCOLM GUITE

The story of the wise men, or "Magi" as Matthew calls them, has a special sense of mystery and joy to it and has long been celebrated by Christians on a special feast day called Epiphany. The Greek word *epipháneia* means "shining out" or "revealing." Of course, the Bible is full of great epiphanies: The burning bush that caused Moses to turn aside and meet God was an epiphany; Isaiah's vision in chapter 6 of "the Lord lifted up" was an epiphany; the heavens opening at Jesus' baptism was an epiphany. So how did this particular moment in Matthew's gospel come to be called the Epiphany? The answer lies in the fact that it is of special importance to us who are of Gentile descent—those who were not born into the Jewish race, the original chosen people.

Sometimes, reading the Old Testament feels like overhearing someone else's long family history, and it makes you wonder what it really has to do with you. But then suddenly you hear your own name and realize this is your story too. This is what happens in the moment that the Magi reach the Jesus child. Until now, the story of the coming Messiah has been confined to Israel, the covenant people, but here suddenly and mysteriously, three Gentiles have intuited that his birth is good news for them too and brought gifts accordingly. Here is an epiphany, a revelation, that the birth of Christ is not one small step for a local religion but a great leap for all mankind. Jesus is for all of us, Gentile and Jew alike!

I love the way that the three wise men are traditionally depicted as representing the different races, cultures, and languages of the world. I love the way the world, in all its diversity, is captured in the Magi's character of diligence and joy. They "search diligently," but they rejoice "with exceeding great joy" (Matt. 2:8, 10, KJV). I love the way they follow a star, letting it lead them to something beyond itself. Here's a sonnet that tries to express a little of what this story might mean for us:

It might have been just someone else's story,
Some chosen people get a special king.
We leave them to their own peculiar glory,
We don't belong, it doesn't mean a thing.
But when these three arrive
they bring us with them,
Gentiles like us, their wisdom might be ours;
A steady step that finds an inner rhythm,
A pilgrim's eye that sees beyond the stars.
They did not know his name
but still they sought him,
They came from otherwhere
but still they found;
In temples they found those
who sold and bought him,
But in the filthy stable, hallowed ground.
Their courage gives our questing hearts a voice
To seek, to find, to worship, to rejoice.

This sonnet, "Epiphany," is from *Sounding the Seasons* (Canterbury Press, 2012) and is used with the author's permission.

REFLECT

The combination of diligence and joy displayed by the wise men is notable. Reflecting on their example, how can we cultivate a balance of diligent seeking and joyful rejoicing in our own pursuit of Christ?

READ
REV. 21:1-6

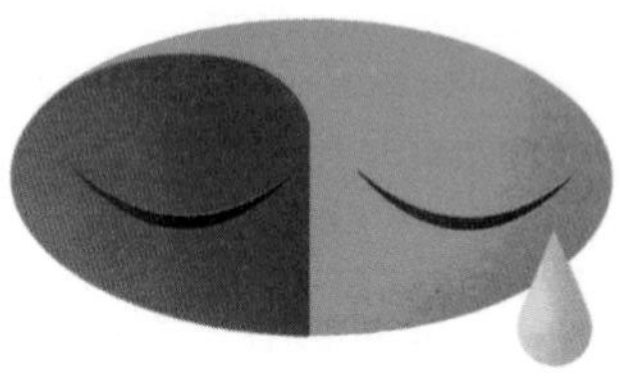

Advent for Grieving Hearts

THE HOPE OF UNION THAT HELPS US PERSEVERE TODAY

BY CRAIG SMITH

The Christmas season isn't always jolly and merry. In fact, it can be filled with heartache, sorrow, tears, and pain. I understand this intimately. Ever since June 30, 2021, my family's holidays have been marked by tears and sadness. On that day, our 20-year-old daughter died in a tragic car accident while we traveled home from vacation together. Within seconds, our firstborn child was taken from us.

Death is our enemy. I hate death—I am tired of tears. And yet, if that June day is my greatest day of sorrow, then Revelation 21 is my greatest source of hope and comfort. It can be yours as well.

In these words, we find the assurance of the eternal victory that Jesus has secured for his people. The loving Shepherd will wipe away our tears and eradicate sin, death, and the devil forevermore. That is our future reward and the destiny of all those who are people of faith.

The scope of the gospel of Jesus Christ isn't limited to the salvation of our souls. It includes the restoration and redemption of all that was lost at the fall of man in Genesis 3. This restoration will involve a new heaven, a new Jerusalem, and perfected bodies that are resurrected to inhabit a glorious new earth. We eagerly await a transformation of the entire universe.

The vision of what is to come, captured in Revelation 21, will be new in quality and superior in character to what we have now. Just as the text predicts this present earth's passing away, it immediately speaks of the ushering in of a new and magnificent beginning. This new earth is the place where Christ's kingdom will be revealed in its fullness, where God himself will reign as the sole King over it all, dwelling in peace and power with his people.

This is the essence of salvation—an intimate, personal relationship with God himself, unending and forevermore. There will be no need for opposing political parties and denominational factions, as we will all be drawn together to worship him, serve him, rule with him, and steward with him. There will be no more death. There will be purposeful work to accomplish, family and friends to enjoy without fear of separation, and an eternity of learning and discovering. It will be a continuous fulfillment of our deepest desire for union with God and each other.

The hope of that great day helps me persevere today, even when the tragedy within our family and the sadness of the holidays feel overwhelming. Our Lord arrived on that first Christmas in great humility, but he will return again in absolute victory. The mighty vision given to the apostle John in the Book of Revelation closes with the Lord saying, "Yes, I am coming soon." To which John responds, along with every sorrowing heart, "Amen. Come, Lord Jesus."

REFLECT

How does the promise of Revelation 21:1–6 provide hope for those grieving during the Christmas season?

How can the anticipation of the new heaven and new earth influence our perspective on today's challenges?

His mercy extends to those who fear him, from generation to generation.

LUKE 1:50